Racer Ronnie: The Friendship Race

Written by Michael Keen,
Jessie Keen, & Sandra Keen

Illustrated by Sandra Keen

Edited by Sandra Keen,
Jennifer Yates, & Cindy Osmer

Keen Inspirational Media™
Be Inspired

ACKNOWLEDGEMENTS

Jessie and Michael would like to dedicate this book to all of their friends. They are blessed with so many good friends that support and encourage them to do their best, even when in competition with each other.

This book is inspired by a competitive experience with one of these amazing friends.

Thanks also to Ronnie Osmer who shared his knowledge of and passion for racing. He is a role model who supports worthy charities, works hard, drives fast, and does what he loves.

My name is Racer Ronnie, and I woke up ready to race today!

Today was my first race in my new Bandolero race car. I knew that I was ready because I had practiced a lot. It was definitely a race to remember.

On my way to the race, I thought about racing in my Bandolero. I also remembered that my friend, Danny, would be racing.

Danny and I always had so much fun practicing together. Sometimes he was faster and sometimes I was faster, but we always finished together. I would be happy if either of us won, but I hoped Danny thought that, too.

I pulled my car up to the starting grid. When they told us to start our engines, I took a deep breath and settled into my seat. I checked my seatbelt, pulled on my gloves, and adjusted my helmet.

I started focusing on the race. I saw Danny line up next to me. I told myself that, even though this was just the heat race, everything would be O.K. We followed the pace car onto the track. When the pace car pulled off and the flagman waved the green flag, the race was on.

When the flagman threw the green flag, I did not get a good start, and I fell to the back of the pack quickly. That was not a good place to be. Once I settled down, I drove my line and quickly started passing up the other cars, one at a time. Finally, I saw my friend in the distance. He was leading the race.

I kept on racing and did not give up. I was able to catch Danny and passed him on the inside.   For the next couple of laps, on each corner, Danny would pass me or I would pass him. I started laughing when we were passing each other, and I hoped he was laughing, too. It was so much fun and was just like we had practiced.

The last few corners were crazy. I got loose in the corner, and my car started to slide. I was able to save it from crashing, but I lost some speed there. I drove too deep into the next corner, and it felt like the car was going to hit the outside wall. That gave Danny the edge he needed.

I tried hard and finished while following him closely. Danny finished the heat race in first place, and I came in second place.

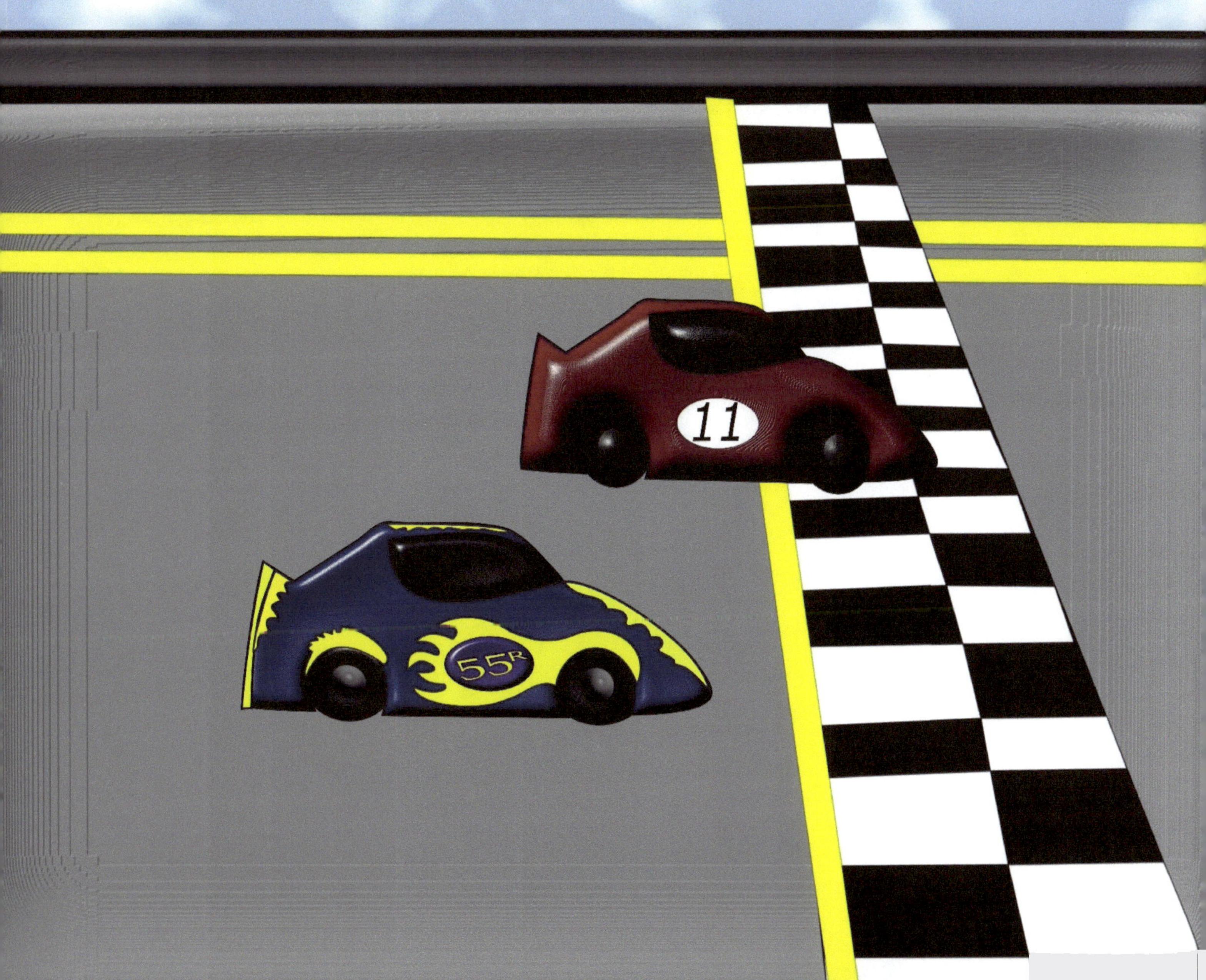

As soon as the heat race was done, we pulled back into the garage so we could make adjustments to the cars before the feature race. Danny got out of his car and came over to talk to me. He had a big smile on his face and yelled to me as he got closer. He said, "I really thought you were going to pass me on that last turn!" I said, "I was really trying, but you took that inside corner and won!" We laughed some more, and I told him he might not be so lucky in the feature race.

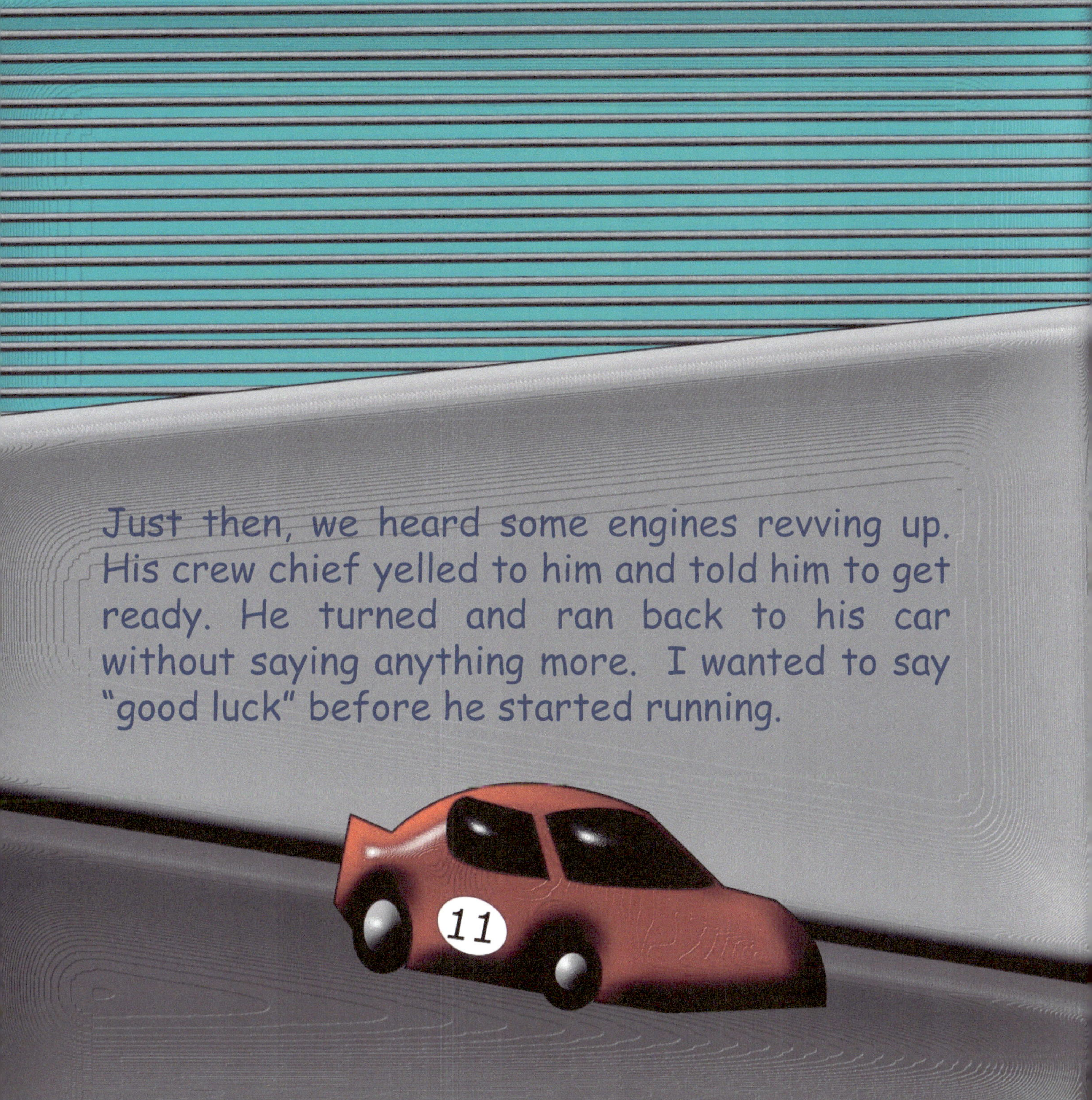

Just then, we heard some engines revving up. His crew chief yelled to him and told him to get ready. He turned and ran back to his car without saying anything more. I wanted to say "good luck" before he started running.

Both of us had good starting positions because we qualified in first and second place. He had an edge, though, because he won the heat race. That made him the "pole sitter."

Once again, I took a deep breath, checked my seatbelt, and I adjusted my gloves and helmet. We followed the pace car back onto the track and waited for the flagman to throw the green flag.

This time, I had a good start. I followed my friend closely on every turn. I was able to do a crossover and pass him, but in the next corner, Danny did a crossover and passed me. It seemed like the car that was in second place going into the corner had the advantage coming out.

We swapped places a lot and were able to stay at the front of the field. We do that a lot in our races. All of a sudden, Danny hit some debris on the track and spun out.

The flagman threw the yellow flag, and the pace car came on the track. The pace car slowed everyone down.

As I made the last turn before the restart, I saw my friend coming back up behind the rest of the pack. His car was not damaged and he was able to regain control and get back in the race, but he had to start at the back of the field.

He spent the rest of the race
catching up with me, just as I had
done during the heat race. He did
not make it easy on me either,
because he did catch up. Both of
us fought for first place again..

I saw the white flag being waved. That meant one lap to go, and I had to do my best. I looked in my mirror and saw Danny coming up behind me on my inside. I moved lower on the track and would not let him pass. Then, I saw Danny move to the outside of my car, so I moved up the track. We were both giving it our best.

I looked up and saw the checkered
flag waving. It was close, and I won!

After the race, Danny gave me a high five and said that he would catch me next time. He was really happy for me. I learned that it is ok to win when racing a friend and that we need our friends to challenge us to be the best that we can be. I'm glad to have good friends, and glad to have friends to race with.

<u>Author's Insights – Michael – Age 11</u>

I got the idea for this story from my cross-country experience because I am not a race car driver. To write this story, I thought about the first time I ran a cross-country race. I love running cross-country races, practicing with my good friends, and running with our cross-country team. I had one friend who always raced a close race with me, and he pushed me to run faster. To tell this story, I wrote about a cross-country race. Then, my brother, Jessie, re-wrote it and made it into a race car driving story. It's easy to write stories when you talk about things you've done.

My friend and I always tried to do our best. We never came in first, but we always finished strong and really did stay together. When we ran our first race together, we kept up with each other from the beginning of the race until the end and pushed each other to keep going. Before the race, we agreed to do our best. In this story, the fictional racers probably should have talked to solve the problem, but that would not have been as fun of a story. So, I guess two lessons came from this story. First, always do your best. Second, talk to your friends when something is bothering you.

Author's Insights - Jessie – Age 13

I enjoyed adapting Michael's cross-country story to be about race cars. I tried to use terms and ideas that I learned when talking with Ronnie Osmer about his racing adventures. I have competed in a lot of competitions and games against friends, like Tae Kwon Do Tournaments, football games, and basketball games.

With every tournament, my friends and I knew that we would do our best and that after the tournament, we would still be great friends with no hard feelings. We encouraged each other. Some of us do things better than others. The cool thing about it is that we can help each other to get better. My friends do that for me, and I hope that they think I do that for them.

MORE TO COME

Learn more about Ronnie Osmer
events and racing at
Ronnieosmer.net
Facebook: Ronnie Osmer Racing

~

Also, enjoy the upcoming releases of the
Racer Ronnie Series of books on amazon.com.

Thank you for reading and for supporting
what we do.

We Love What We Do!

~

Follow us on Facebook
at Keen Inspirational Media for
anticipated release dates
and also for additional titles.
Contact: Sandra@keeninspirationalmedia.com

Other Titles by These Authors

The Friendship Oyster by Sandra Keen
Illustrated by Milton Keen & Sandra Keen

Getting Ready for School: My Morning Routine
By Michael Keen & Sandra Keen
Illustrated by Rosita Henley

A Brothers' Review: Our Day at Universal Orlando
A Visit to Two Parks in One Day
By Jessie, Michael, and Sandra Keen

Get Healthy with Color:
Health Logs and Coloring Art
By Sandra Keen

Racer Ronnie: Racing Terms for Kids
by Jessie, Michael, & Sandra Keen
Illustrated by Sandra Keen

JAX and Allie: Beach Fun
by Sandra Keen
Illustrated by Melissa Keen

Other Anticipated Titles

A Brothers' Review: New Orleans
By Jessie, Michael, and Sandra Keen

A Brothers' Review: The Road to Washington
By Jessie, Michael, Milton and Sandra Keen

Racer Ronnie: The Championship Race
By Jessie, Michael, and Sandra Keen
Illustrated by Bruce Trascher & Sandra Keen

About Racer Ronnie

by Jessie Keen

Racer Ronnie is a racing book series based on a real race car driver named Ronnie Osmer. Actually, Racer Ronnie is a nickname that was given to him by his friends.

Ronnie Osmer was 7 years old when he started racing. He first started racing go carts and has raced six different kinds of cars during his racing career. Ronnie is currently starting his senior year in high school.

Ronnie has a passion for racing, and his favorite car is "any Corvette." Ronnie's other hobbies include basketball, football, golf, and soccer. He played on many of his grammar school and high school teams. Among many racing victories, he has won two Championships at Sunny South Raceway, and also won the Legends Louisiana State Championship. He makes personal appearances at car shows and supports a number of charities.

Ronnie races with the number 55 in honor of his favorite racer, Michael Waltrip, and added a small "R" to make it his own. His dad is his Crew Chief. He is also supported and encouraged by his mom and dad in all of his competitions.

About the Authors

Jessie

Jessie is a 13 year old entering the 8th Grade. He loves to play flag football and basketball. He is a 3rd Degree level 1 Black Belt in Tae Kwon Do. He also likes running, swimming, watching movies, and spending time with friends and family. Other favorite activities include grilling with Dad, throwing the football with Mom, playing video games with his brother and visiting with his grandparents.

Michael

Michael is an 11 year old entering 6th Grade. He loves to play the trumpet and listen to music. Basketball is his favorite sport. He also runs on his school's cross-country team. He is a 1st degree level 2 Black Belt in Tae Kwon Do. Michael loves to swim, play video games and spend time with friends and family. Michael is also a car enthusiast and is full of facts about a wide range of vehicles.

Sandra

Sandra is a mom with a background in healthcare business management and business writing. She enjoys spending time with family while swimming, watching movies, and working on family projects like this. Writing with Jessie and Michael began as a family project to help the boys with daily writing structure. It's turned into a much more enjoyable family experience.